Inventing the Americas

poems by

William Heath

Finishing Line Press
Georgetown, Kentucky

Inventing the Americas

ACKNOWLEDGMENTS

"The Death of Marco Polo," *Arlington Literary Journal*

With thanks Frank and Holly Bergon, Marty Malone, David Salner, and
above all and as always my wife Roser Caminals-Heath for reading the
manuscript and offering invaluable advice.

Publisher: Leah Huete de Maines
Editor: Christen Kincaid
Cover Art: "Discovery of America," designed by Johannes Stradanus,
engraved by Theodore Galle, later colorized. Creative Commons CCO 1.0
Universal Public Domain Dedication
Author Photo: Josep Caminals
Cover Design: Elizabeth Maines McCleavy

Order online: www.finishinglinepress.com
also available on amazon.com
and abebooks.com

Author inquiries and mail orders:
Finishing Line Press
PO Box 1626
Georgetown, Kentucky 40324
USA

Contents

For Marty Malone
Good friend and fellow poet

The Death of Marco Polo

An uneasy priest come
to administer last rites
admonishes Marco Polo
to confess his sins,
tell the truth about
his celebrated travels.
Everyone knows he has
exaggerated the facts,
told extravagant falsehoods
and fabulous tales of
golden cities in the East.
Surely he must set
the record straight here
before the eyes of men,
in the presence of God.
Marco motions the good
father to lean closer,
and, mustering what
strength he has left,
whispers loudly enough
for all to hear: *I have
not told the half of it!*

Construing the Globe

Every place he goes Cristóbal Colón
carries a copy of Marco Polo's *Travels*.
Aristotle and other Greek thinkers
knew the earth was round, as did
the informed of 15th-century Europe.
The key questions are how large
the globe, the ratio of land to water,
how far to the golden roofs of Cathay,
can ships sailing west reach
the kingdom of the Great Khan.

Since the 1453 sack of Constantinople
the spice trade along the Silk Road
and across the Black Sea has shrunk
to a trickle. The times demand
a new route to the riches of the East.
Toscanelli, a wise man of Florence,
argues the spice islands off the coast
of Japan are within sailing range.
Bristol and Basque fishermen may
already know of strange shores.

For years Colón sails the Mediterranean,
talks with veteran sailors, learns
to navigate by astrolabe and compass;
he believes an apocryphal verse
in *Esdra: Six parts hast thou dried up;*
he ponders Plato's account of Atlantis,
a lost continent past the Pillars of Hercules,
Seneca's prophecy of a vast land beyond
a remote emerald isle known as Thule.

He visits Bristol to pry into the secret
lair of the bountiful cod fisheries—
now the Grand Banks of Newfoundland.
In Galway a small boat drifts in
holding a man and a woman, dead
from exposure, with straight black hair
and slanted eyes. Colón knows nothing
of the Inuit and other Artic people,
assumes they are Chinese.

Isabella's Permission

His schemes shunned by other countries
for seven years Colón seeks the aid of Spain.
Isabella orders Hernando de Talavera
to form a commission of learned men
to say if the plan merits royal approval.

Church scholars gather in Salamanca
for never-ending debates.
Colón boasts before the court
that he alone can find the riches
of the East by sailing west.

The commission finds *colossal errors*
in Colón's project: it is *impossible*
and vain and worthy of rejection.
The western ocean is *infinite*
and probably unnavigable, any fool

attempting such a voyage, even if
the ships reach the Antipodes, will not
be able to sail back again, any lands
found would be worthless, otherwise
why would our Lord hide them?

My proposition was a thing of mockery,
Colón complains, *all who learned of*
my plan made merry at my expense.
In spite of the bigotry and stupidity
on display, Colón's calculations

are deeply flawed: the Orient is
five times further away than he thinks.
His arrogance offends Ferdinand,
yet Isabella sympathizes, does not
reject him, offers a final chance.

Once Granada, last Moorish stronghold,
falls in 1492, the queen grants royal support.
In the "Capitulations" Colón demands
fancy titles for himself and his heirs,
the power to rule, a tenth of the profits.

1492 is a fateful year: seeking unity,
Spain imposes uniformity; a nation
in need of cross-cultural understanding
and expertise, drives the Moors
out of Andalucía, expels the Jews.

Colón's three ships: *Niña* (the girl), *Pinta*
(the painted one), *Marigalante* (Fancy Mary),
have sailors' names for portside prostitutes.
The latter is rechristened *Santa María*.
The New World saga of misnaming begins.

Outward Bound

Colón has a notion
the earth is one large land mass,
like a great hand gripping a ball
it covers most of the globe.
He doesn't foresee continents
blocking his way to the East.

He keeps two copies of his logs,
one to show the sailors, one
for their true position (or so
he thinks). The phony entries
are better, the size of the world
belies his charts.

Lost in an immense ocean,
the poor sailors gnaw
maggoty biscuits, drink rancid
wine, sing the *Salve Regina*,
no choice but to follow the dream
of their half-crazed captain.

Then come days like
April in Andalucía, the calm
sea like the river in Sevilla,
Rodrigo de Triana the first
to cry out, "*Tierra! Tierra!*"
never gets the promised

reward of a silken doublet.
Colón sees green trees,
naked natives, believes
he has arrived at
an archipelago of the Indies
off the coast of Japan.

The resolute captain is sure
around the next cape he'll find
cities of gold, precious stones,
the kingdom of the Great Khan.
The world in his head
is not the one under his feet.

The First Day

Picture this: Colón steps
on shore, a small table
is set up in the sand, a scribe
draws up documents taking
possession in the name of Spain
of the said island the natives
call Guanahaní, isle of iguanas,
now misnamed San Salvador.

What gives Colón the right?
If he's in the Indies don't
these islands belong to
the Great Khan or some
other Eastern potentate?
Yet the natives are naked,
private parts barely covered,
what rights can they have?

There it is in pen and paper,
a testament to who owns what,
signed with lavish flourishes.
Next comes a gift exchange,
hawkbells, glass beads, trinkets
of little value which provide
great pleasure to *a people
very poor in everything.*

The natives are well built,
in good health, open, friendly,
intelligent, and amenable:
Colón assumes they could
more easily *be converted
to our holy faith by love
than by force since* [no priests
in sight] *they had no religion.*

They are not as dark
as the Canary islanders
or as light as Europeans.
Faces and bodies painted
many colors, some red,
some white, yet Colón
does not relate this to
any system of belief.

Their weapons are bows
and arrows, sharpened sticks
tipped by a fish's tooth,
they know nothing of iron.
When he displays his sword
one grasps it by the blade,
cuts his hand, the first blood
shed by Spanish steel.

Colón concludes:
naked people must be inferior;
not knowing the value of things
they are easily deceived;
strong healthy bodies, quick minds,
and lack of arms fit them
to be slaves; he takes ten captives
so *that they may learn to speak.*

It's all there on the first day:
an empire in the making,
the millions that will die.

The First Voyage

Colón reports that the people believe
he and his men have descended from Heaven,
maybe not divine, just visitors from the sky.
Either way the natives are so timid
his men could subdue any resistance.

Colón notes lushly green tall trees
laden with tasty fruits, a fertile land,
the singing of flocks of exotic birds,
special praise for the spectacular colors
of parrots of numerous kinds.

Nothing beckons as urgently as gold.
The smallest ring in the nose
of a native whets his passion to find
more. The villagers possess long dugouts
that can cross open water to a place
rich in gold called Cuba, which sounds
to him like Cipango, Japan.

The inhabitants of the islands
fear a warlike people they call Caribs
who raid, take captives, kill them,
roast and eat their flesh. These
dread Caribs must be soldiers
fighting for the Great Khan,
the riches of the East must be near.

A boy left at the tiller falls asleep,
Colón's treasured flagship hits
a reef, runs aground on a sandbar,
crashing waves soon open the planks,
the men rush to unload the cargo
before the foundering vessel sinks.
Colón is convinced the disaster
is for the best, the Lord intends

for him to settle at this place, build
houses and a fort beside the bay
next to a large village whose
headman promises friendship.

Since the wreck happens on
Christmas Eve, Colón names the town
La Navidad. Some forty of the crew
agree to stay. Timid males, naked females,
the prospect of gold—what could go wrong?
Colón vows to return within a year.

Triumphal Return

Colón instructs the men at *La Navidad*
to build a strong fort and maintain good
relations with the people of the village.
As proof of Spanish power he fires
a cannon before his two ships depart.

At one island the natives are hostile,
in a brief skirmish a warrior
is slashed in the buttocks, another
shot in the chest with a crossbow
is the first to die in combat.

On the return voyage Colón sails
for so many miles along the coast
of Cuba he is sure it is a continent,
perhaps a province of Cathay—
the Indians insist it is a large island.

Despite tempest-tossed seas,
gale-force winds and contrary currents,
Colón docks at Cascaes near Lisbon.
Portugal debates having him killed,
decides to treat him honorably.

In a letter to Ferdinand and Isabella,
Colón celebrates his discoveries.
A copy reaches Rome; translated
and printed in Latin it is read
in Europe among a select few.

Colón promises the king and queen
that with their assistance he can
give them as much gold as they
have need of...as many human slaves
as their majesties choose to demand.

He has discovered the unknown.
For if anyone has written or told anything
about these islands, all have done so
either obscurely or by guess work,
so that it has seemed to be fabulous.

Colón arrives in Sevilla on Palm Sunday.
In Barcelona he leads a procession—
followed by his Taino captives holding
a rainbow array of parrots in cages—
to meet with the king and queen.

What the "Capitulations" promised
comes to pass. Colón has discovered
rich lands for Spain that his descendants
will govern in perpetuity. His title
is now "*Admiral of the Ocean Sea.*"

The Second Voyage

This time Colón has full royal support.
Seventeen ships, twelve hundred colonists,
priests, hidalgos, soldiers, men to mine
and assess the gold. Horses, farm animals,
but no women. Most plan to get rich,
return to Spain.

They sail from Cádiz in late September,
make landfall in early November, on sight
the natives flee into the thick woods.
At La Navidad Colón fires two cannons,
receives no response, the fort's palisade,
all the houses burned to the ground.

A search uncovers mangled corpses
strewn in the weeds, the stark truth:
the forty men left there are dead.
They took women for their pleasure,
tortured people for more gold,
the Tainos killed them in revenge.

Colón founds a new town, *Isabela*,
where the colonists repeat
the blunders of their countrymen
on a far larger scale. Each man
claims his own concubines,
imposes a tax in gold.

Those who do not produce
a thimble-sized hawkbell of gold
every three months have their hands
cut off. The natives are forced
to mine for gold in the mountains
work as serfs in the hot fields.

Since the Tainos are heathens,
not pagans, the priests convert them.
To honor Christ and his apostles,
miscreants guilty of backsliding
or other crimes are publicly
hanged in batches of thirteen.

Six Tainos are seen burying
religious icons in a corn field,
pissing on them; put on trial,
they are burned at the stake
for simply using Christian
magic to fertilize their crops.

Colón is a mariner, no governor.
He leaves his brother Diego
in charge at Isabela where chaos
and cruelty rule. Disillusioned settlers
return to Spain, native rebels
are mercilessly crushed.

At sea, Colón discovers Jamaica,
returns to Cuba. He makes his crew
swear a solemn oath that the coast
is the Asian mainland—no one dares
deny what he could not know on pain
of having his tongue cut out.

Without enough profit in gold
to satisfy an insatiable thirst,
the Spaniards ship slaves to Spain.
Four hundred of the most fit Tainos
are packed below deck. Half die
in the crossing, tossed overboard.
Sharks follow the ship's wake.

Thousands of natives perish
by the sword; lacking immunity
against the Black Death and other
plagues that have long ravaged Europe,
far more die from disease.

No matter the good or ill intentions
of the colonists most natives are doomed
to succumb to the invisible—microbes
will kill millions. In less than
a century the Tainos are extinct.

The Third Voyage

Humbled by the hardships
he has endured, Colón returns
to Spain in the ashen habit
of a Franciscan friar. Fallen from
royal favor, this time he scrapes up
six ships and a crew of convicts.

At the first island he sees a trio
of mountains, names it *La Trinidad.*
Some ships stop at Santo Domingo,
latest launching point and cockpit
of Spanish imperialism, while Colón

ventures on with the other three
to make new discoveries. Along
the coast of Venezuela four
mighty freshwater rivers
surge into the salt sea.

These are mouths of the Orinoco
pouring into the Gulf of Paria,
but to Colón they are a mystery
that tests his conflicted worldview
based on contrary authorities.

So great a river can only mean
a mainland, perhaps a continent.
In support he cites *Esdras,*
book four, chapter six:
most of the earth is dry land.

This apocryphal source has
the approval of Church Fathers
St. Ambrose and St. Augustine.
In addition, he listens to Indians
who speak of a rich mainland.

As a veteran navigator
his empirical side knows that
so much fresh water can only
mean a huge land mass,
a fact the natives confirm.

Yet in Colón's mind experience
yields to religious beliefs
seasoned by medieval mysticism.
Genesis says that four rivers
ran out of the Garden of Eden.

He notes the natives are *whiter*
than others and live near the Equator
where the best authorities agree
Paradise would be found. This land
called *Paria* must be that place.

The earth is not round, Colón declares
but *has the shape of a pear,*
prominent at the stem, *like a woman's*
nipple, a place nearest to the sky
and site of the *Terrestrial Paradise.*

Your Majesty I have just found
the Garden of Eden he writes
to the queen—no need of proof,
he makes no effort to explore
the river to its mythic headwaters.

A royal emissary in Santo Domingo
witnesses seven Spaniards hanging
from gallows in the town square.
Although his brother's misrule is at fault,
Colón is blamed, sent home in chains.

In his *Book of Prophecies* he reveals
the esoteric mission encoded in his name:
Cristóbal Colón can only mean
St. Christopher the Christ Bearer
and Colón the ordained colonizer.

In Santo Domingo he is called
"The Admiral of Mosquitoes."

The Final Voyage

A crew of dissolute old salts,
teenage boys, four worm-eaten caravels.
Two make it across the ocean.
Banned from Santo Domingo,
he sails the coast of Venezuela
seeking a passage to the Indies.

Colón's ship wrecks on a remote
Jamaican shore. Two hundred miles
from any help, he and his men
are stranded for a year.
Thirty-two die, Colón and the rest,
gravely ill, long for death.

In a makeshift vessel built
from rotten wood, rusty nails,
shirts for sails, they reach Panama,
well cultivated, densely populated,
where people dress in cotton,
wear golden ornaments.

The natives tell of far more gold
in a vast kingdom to the south,
take him to inspect a sepulcher
large as a house of sculpted stone—
an early intimation of the Inca,
Maya, and Aztec empires.

Finding passage on a sturdy ship,
the men survive furious hurricanes
and return safely to Andalucía.
Colón is unable to see the queen,
who will die in three weeks.

Colón is now a broken man
with bloodshot eyes, aching
limbs, his sufferings rival
Job's: *I am wholly ruined,*
may Heaven have pity on me,
let the earth weep for me.

He believes his divine mission
is complete, he has given Spain
another world (*otro mundo*)
hitherto unknown, keys to open
the Ocean Sea, power to possess
new lands of untold wealth.

Colón's obsession with gold endures:
Gold is treasure, he who possesses it
does all he wishes in this world.
His dream is to restore Jerusalem;
instead Spain squanders its wealth
on imperial follies.

He dies in Valladolid a few
years later, a forgotten man.
The new world he has discovered
does not even bear his name.

Simonetta Vespucci

Like Colón, she is born in Genoa,
at age fifteen comes to Florence.
Her lovely looks draw all eyes,
Amerigo's cousin Marco
weds the *Queen of Beauty.*

Next door lives a family of tanners,
(never mind the penetrating odors),
one of the sons, known to us
as Botticelli, makes her his model
for several masterpieces.

Most notably *The Birth of Venus*—
the goddess is wafted toward shore
on a scallop shell, her body
veiled by long golden tresses,
two hands to protect her modesty.

The Birth of Venus embodies
the spirit of the Renaissance,
she rises from the Mediterranean Sea
with the promise of new worlds
avid to disclose their wonders.

Amerigo helps commission
a painting by Piero di Cosimo
where she appears bare-breasted,
a serpent circling her neck.
All of Florence is smitten.

When tuberculosis takes her
at twenty-three, the grief-stricken
city carries her open coffin
through the streets to offer
a last glimpse of her face.

Leonardo da Vinci, part of
the cortege, draws a final sketch.
The most beautiful woman
of her time and place is dead,
Poets pen her elegy.

Amerigo Vespucci

Eons ago the earth's plates shift,
separate the hemispheres, an ocean
yawns in the middle. Three continents
meet at the Mediterranean whose cities
are the fount of Western civilization.

The European discovery of the New World
centers on the Caribbean, where two
continents meet and native cultures thrive.
The saga of exploration and conquest is
the reuniting of these two facing seas.

A playmate of Amerigo in Florence
is Piero de' Medici, son of Lorenzo
the Magnificent. The Vespucci are
an established family and Amerigo
is well-schooled in the Humanities.

As a young man he works for the Medici,
is settled in Sevilla for Colón's
triumphal return in 1493; he helps
outfit his seventeen-ship fleet; in Triana
taverns he hears sailors tell their tales.

Tired of his dockside job, hungering
for his share of fame and adventure—
I prepared myself to go and observe
a part of the world and its wonders—
he sets sail from Cádiz in May 1499.

His captain, Alonzo de Ojeda of Cuenca,
reaches the West Indies and divides
his ships; Amerigo, sailing southward,
sees Venezuela, the huge Gulf of Paria,
fresh waters spewing from the Amazon.

He is enraptured by the sweet
singing of brightly colored birds,
the fragrance of an infinite variety of
foliage, fruits, and flowers, the temperate
climate and friendly naked people.

*We thought perhaps we had entered
the Earthly Paradise,* but an inferno
awaits—along the coast they fight
hostile natives *innumerable times,*
kill hundreds, burn their homes.

The Caribs are not the ony cannibals,
other mainland tribes often raid
villages of their enemies, take prisoners,
feast on their flesh. In some houses
limbs are hung to smoke like hams.

On a return stop in the Bahamas
they relish the natives' weakness,
we did what we liked with them,
capture 232 as slaves, in Cádiz sell
the 200 that survive the voyage.

In 1502 Amerigo joins a Portuguese
expedition to Brazil. For several weeks
he lives among the Tupi, a well-built
people with long black hair, no beards.
facial punctures for bones and stones.

Once more he is impressed by
the sights, sounds, and smells
of a verdant world with no king
to obey, *each is his own master,*
everything is shared in common,

including women eager to please
these bearded men from the sky.
Everyone sleeps in woven nets
suspended in the air. In spite of
fierce enemies, they live long lives.

A New World

Amerigo sends letters about his adventures
to his boyhood friends in Florence.
Upon his return from his second voyage
to celebrate the new world's wonders
he writes in Latin *Mundus Novus.*

This popular pamphlet creates a sensation
in Europe by its depiction of
the alluring and appalling. Far more
than Colón's letters he captures
the imagination of readers.

Unlike the lands Colón thinks
he has found, Amerigo insists
his discoveries are separate from Asia.
They belong to a new continent
in an unknown quarter of the globe.

Amerigo becomes the Botticelli
of a Caribbean Sea whose Venuses
are beautiful, desirable, available,
and skilled in the ways of the flesh
to satisfy the most *inordinate lust.*

Decency bids us pass over the details,
yet he implies a potion or poison
is used to enlarge the male penis.
Plus a man can relax on fine cotton
as a hammock sways in the breeze.

In addition to a sensuous Eden
of sexual gratification, Amerigo
portrays a *golden world without toil:*
kings and laws replaced by liberty,
equality, harmony, abundance.

In this Paradise custom-made
to fulfill male fantasies,
there are no priests, no religion,
people live together in large houses,
nobody covets another's goods.

Mundus Novus provides an antidote
to the divine right of monarchs,
strictures of church doctrine,
privileges of an entrenched aristocracy,
the hierarchies of feudalism.

Venturing into the dense jungle
Amerigo is startled by an anaconda
and fearsome crocodiles, yet
a more deadly specter lurks in
this Edenic garden—cannibalism:

A handsome, well-built Portuguese,
admired by several women, suddenly
is clubbed to death on the spot,
dragged off, roasted over a fire,
cut into pieces, eaten in triumph.

Europeans use such horrors
to justify future brutalities.
Victims of the Inquisition
are burned alive; the Tupi wait
until their enemies are dead.

The sensationalism of *Mundus Novus,*
its captivating blend of information
and outlandish fiction make a deep
impression on the Renaissance mind,
his lurid version has a lasting impact.

When a German cartographer draws
a map of a newly expanded globe
a poet friend suggests that because
a fourth part has been discovered
by Amerigo, its name should be *America.*

And *America* it remains, a land
where fact and fantasy merge,
and true histories are trumped
by pleasing myths.

William Heath has published four poetry books: *The Walking Man, Steel Valley Elegy, Going Places* and *Alms for Oblivion;* two chapbooks, *Night Moves in Ohio* and *Inventing the Americas;* three novels: *The Children Bob Moses Led* (winner of the Hackney Award), *Devil Dancer,* and *Blacksnake's Path;* a work of history, *William Wells and the Struggle for the Old Northwest* (winner of two Spur Awards and the Oliver Hazard Perry Award); and a collection of interviews, *Conversations with Robert Stone.* He lives in Annapolis. www.williamheathbooks.com